OF DANGEROUS FOOD

ЯEBVIK

Tate Publishing

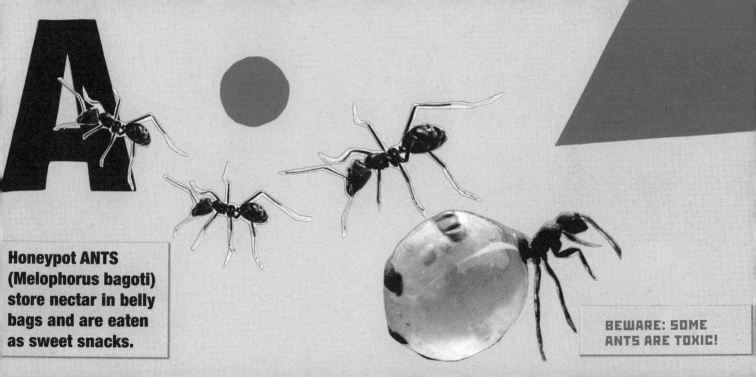

A

Honeypot ANTS (Melophorus bagoti) store nectar in belly bags and are eaten as sweet snacks.

BEWARE: SOME ANTS ARE TOXIC!

B

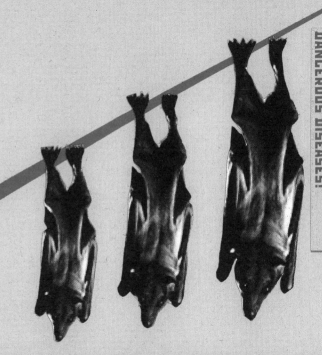

Fruit BATS (Pteropus) are eaten stewed or grilled.

BEWARE: MANY SPECIES ARE ENDANGERED AND SOME CARRY DANGEROUS DISEASES!

C

CROCODILE (Crocodylus) tails are cooked slowly as steaks, stews or curries.

D

DURIAN (Durio zibethinus) is a custard-tasting fruit eaten in biscuits, sweets, rice & curries.

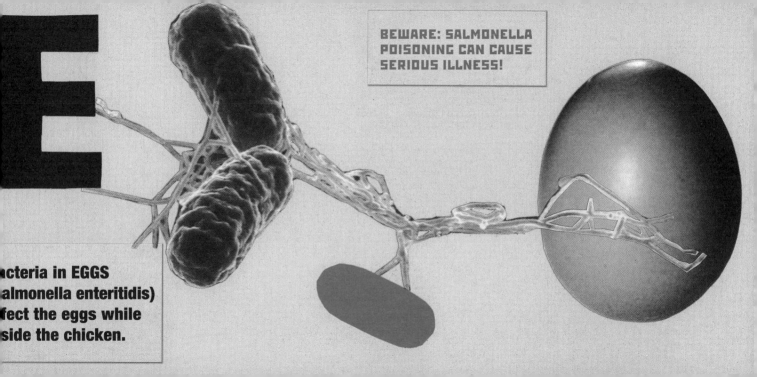

E

cteria in EGGS
almonella enteritidis)
fect the eggs while
side the chicken.

FUGU or Porcupinefish (Diodon Holocanthus) can only be eaten if sliced very carefully by trained chefs.

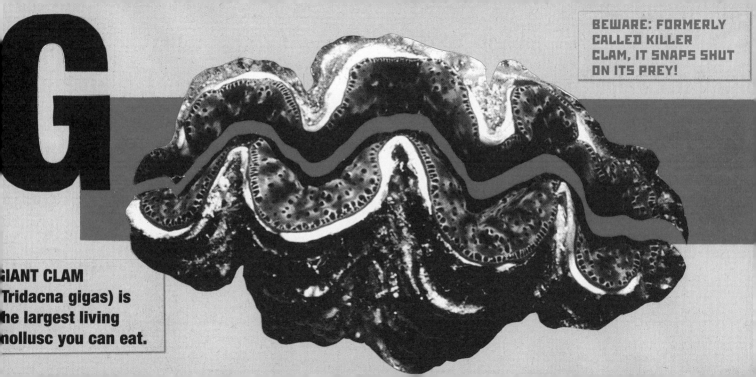

G

GIANT CLAM
(Tridacna gigas) is
the largest living
mollusc you can eat.

H

HEMLOCK (Conium maculatum) can be used in tiny amounts as medicine.

BEWARE: ALL PLANT PARTS ARE DEADLY POISONOUS!

ICE CREAM (Catillamen glaciale) is made from milk, cream, eggs & sugar.

J

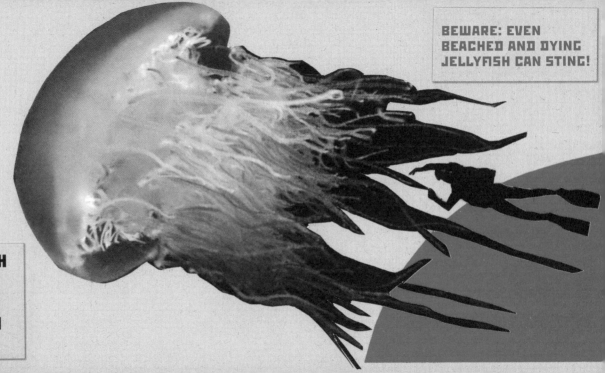

Nomura's **JELLYFISH** (Nemopilema nomurai) are eaten raw, cooked, salted and in cookies.

BEWARE: EVEN BEACHED AND DYING JELLYFISH CAN STING!

K

KROKI (Notesthes robusta) or Bullrout will eat anything that fits in its mouth.

BEWARE: CAMOUFLAGED POISONOUS SPINES INFLICT INTENSE PAIN!

Many LARVAE are eaten worldwide. Diamphidia aren't but are used by hunters to poison arrows.

M

MOULD (Penicillium glaucum) bacteria in blue cheese makes it stinky but tasty.

N

Deadly NIGHTSHADE (Atropa belladonna) is used as a drug in tiny doses.

O

OYSTER (Ostreidae) has been eaten since prehistoric times.

P

POTATO (Solanum
tuberosum) is eaten
boiled, chipped and
roasted all over
the world.

QUERCUS (Oak tree) seeds can be ground for acorn coffee.

BEWARE: LEAVES AND ACORNS ARE POISONOUS IN LARGE AMOUNTS!

R

**RATTLESNAKE
(Crotalus) can be
grilled or eaten raw.**

BEWARE: SNAKE
BITE AND VENOM
CAN BE FATAL!

S

arantula SPIDERS
heraphosidae) make
crispy fried snack.

T

TOADSTOOL (Amanita muscaria) can be eaten carefully prepared.

U

BEWARE: THE SPINES CAN INFLICT A PAINFUL WOUND!

Sea URCHIN (Diadema antillarum) and roe can be eaten raw.

BEWARE: TOO MUCH FLUORIDE IS BAD FOR YOU!

WILLIAUMITE (Sodium Fluoride, NaF) is a mineral used in treated water and toothpaste.

W

WOLFSBANE (Aconitum lycoctonum) has been used in traditional medicine since ancient times.

X

XIPHIUS GLAVIUS (Swordfish) is eaten sliced and grilled as steaks.

Y

Yellow 6 (E110) is a food additive used to colour drinks, jellies, jams, sweets, or packet sauces.

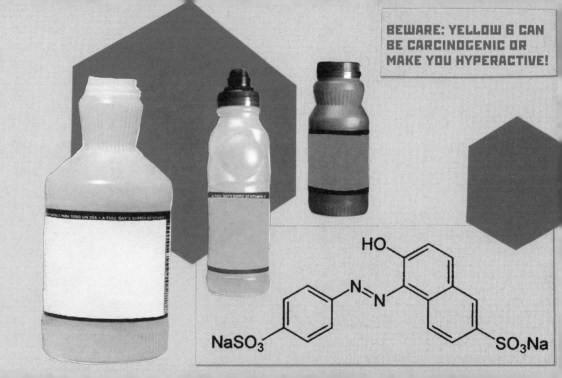

A FULL DAY'S SUPPLY OF VITAMIN C

VITAMINA C PARA TODO UN DÍA • A FULL DAY'S SUPPLY OF VITAMIN

HO

N=N

NaSO$_3$

SO$_3$Na

Z

ZOMBIE: A cocktail made from fruit juices and 3 types of rum, which can be set on fire.

BEWARE: ONE GLASS MAY TURN YOU INTO ONE!

Photocredits

Rebvik is a creative partnership between Rebecca Sinker and Victoria de Rijke, who have been collaborating on projects and publications exploring art, education and play since 1996.

First published 2012 by order of the Tate Trustees
by Tate Publishing, a division of Tate Enterprises Ltd,
Millbank, London SW1P 4RG
www.tate.org.uk/publishing

A catalogue record for this book is available from the British Library
ISBN 978 1 84976 016 4

Distributed in the United States and Canada by ABRAMS, New York
Library of Congress Control Number: applied for

Colour reproduction by Evergreen Colour Separation Co. Ltd, Hong Kong
Printed in China by Toppan Leefung Printing Ltd

MIX
Paper from
responsible sources
FSC® C104723